# Introduction

Decades is the first in a series of books, created specifically for use with people with dementia. The purpose of these books is to encourage reminiscence, provide an enjoyable activity and act as an aid to conversation and communication.

We hope that the books will be used to facilitate group reminiscence in care homes or day centres as well as a shared experience with family and friends.

Covering life in Britain from the 1940's to the 1960's, we have chosen imagery that reflects life from this period in a memorable and positive way.

With a good cross section of subject matter, we hope this book will bring back happy memories such as the Queen's Coronation, sporting achievements, holidays and the stars of cinema and television. Shared national identity in World War Two and the images and everyday items of that dramatic period in our nation's history. Recognizable faces from the past, reflected in fashion, transport, music, housing and familiar product packaging.

With a variety of colourful illustrations we have also included black and white pages intended for colouring, bringing to life people past and memories shared.

# Contents

Written and illustrated by Les Ives
Published by Les Ives Illustration and Publishing © 2014
Print reference number 43242

# Hollywood and film

Odeon cinema

Clark Gable and Vivien Leigh
in "Gone with the Wind"

Judy Garland in "The Wizard of Oz"

Fred Astaire and Ginger Rogers

# Hollywood and film

Micky Mouse in "Fantasia"

Trevor Howard and Celia
Johnson in "Brief Encounter"

Humphrey Bogart and Katharine
Hepburn in "The African Queen"

Alfred Hitchcock
and "The Birds"

# 1940's

RAF Spitfire

Winston Churchill

Anderson bomb shelter

Dig for Victory poster

# 1940's

Home Guard soldier

Evacuee children

Factory girl

Land girls

# 1940's

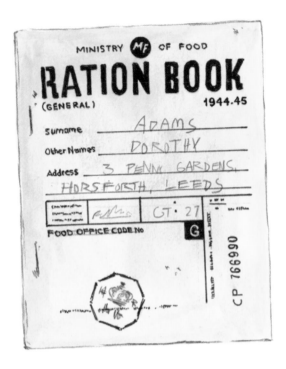

Ration book

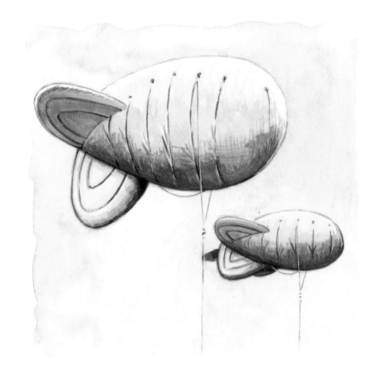

Barrage Balloons

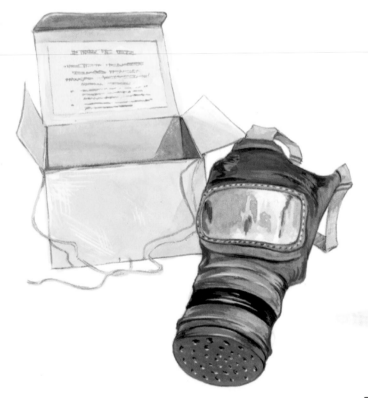

Gas mask and box

Powdered milk and powdered egg

# 1940's

Glenn Miller

Vera Lynn

Wartime radio

VE Day May 8th, 1945

# 1940's Street

AIR-RAID SHELTER

# 1950's

The Queen's coronation 1953

Edmund Hillary climbs
Mount Everest 1953

Roger Bannister runs the
first four minute mile 1954

Prime Minister
Harold Macmillan

# 1950's

Holidays

Big city smog

Washing mangle

Kitchen toaster

# 1950's

Elvis Presley

Marilyn Monroe

Liz Taylor

TV show "Dixon of Dock Green"

# 1950's

Children's TV
character Andy Pandy

Radio stars the "Goons"

Morris Minor

Chocolate and "Spangles" sweets

# 1950's

National Service
soldier

Nurse

Policeman

# 1950's

Teddy boys and girls

# 1960's

Supersonic airliner
"Concorde"

E Type Jaguar

Donald Campbell and
"Bluebird" 1967

Neil Armstrong is the first man
on the moon 1969

# 1960's

Prime Minister Harold Wilson

American President
John F Kennedy

England win the World Cup 1966

Henry Cooper and Cassius Clay

# 1960's

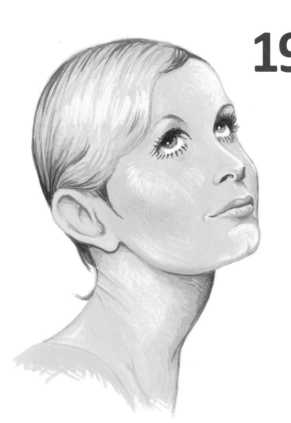

Fashion model Twiggy

Entertainer Cilla Black

Mods and their scooters

Miniskirt fashion

# 1960's

The Beatles

The hippies

Morecambe and Wise

Kitchen products Fairy Liquid
and OMO washing powder

1960's Carnaby Street

21